# Follow Me!

## The Story of Jesus and His Twelve Helpers

We are grateful to the following team of authors for their contributions to *God Loves Me*, a Bible story program for young children. This Bible story, one of a series of fifty-two, was written by Patricia L. Nederveld, managing editor for CRC Publications. Suggestions for using this book were developed by Jesslyn DeBoer, a freelance author from Grand Rapids, Michigan. Yvonne Van Ee, an early childhood educator, served as project consultant and wrote *God Loves Me*, the program guide that accompanies this series of Bible storybooks.

Nederveld has served as a consultant to Title I early childhood programs in Colorado. She has extensive experience as a writer, teacher, and consultant for federally funded preschool, kindergarten, and early childhood programs in Colorado, Texas, Michigan, Florida, Missouri, and Washington, using the *High/Scope* Education Research Foundation curriculum. In addition to writing the *Bible Footprints* church curriculum for four- and five-year-olds, Nederveld edited the revised *Threes* curriculum and the first edition of preschool through second grade materials for the *LiFE* curriculum, all published by CRC Publications.

DeBoer has served as a church preschool leader and as coauthor of the preschool-kindergarten materials for the *LiFE* curriculum published by CRC Publications. She has also written K-6 science and health curriculum for Christian Schools International, Grand Rapids, Michigan, and inspirational gift books for Zondervan Publishing House.

Van Ee is a professor and early childhood program advisor in the Education Department at Calvin College, Grand Rapids, Michigan. She has served as curriculum author and consultant for Christian Schools International and wrote the original *Story Hour* organization manual and curriculum materials for fours and fives.

Photo on page 5: Mike Timo/Tony Stone Images; photo on page 20: Ken Fisher/Tony Stone Images.

**Library of Congress Cataloging-in-Publication Data**

Nederveld, Patricia L., 1944-
     Follow me: the story of Jesus and his twelve helpers/Patricia
L. Nederveld.
       p.  cm. — (God loves me; bk. 29)
     Summary: Follow me! is the call Jesus gave to the twelve men
he chose to be his disciples. They left their work and families
to follow Jesus. Includes follow-up activities.
    ISBN 1-56212-298-3
    1. Jesus Christ—Calling of the twelve—Juvenile literature.
I. Title. II. Series: Nederveld, Patricia L., 1944- God loves me; bk. 29.
BT360.N43  1998
232.9'5—dc21                            97-53317
                                            CIP
                                            AC

10 9 8 7 6 5 4 3 2 1

# Follow Me!

## The Story of Jesus and His Twelve Helpers

PATRICIA L. NEDERVELD

ILLUSTRATIONS BY CATHY ANN JOHNSON

CRC Publications
Grand Rapids, Michigan

This is a story
from God's
book, the Bible.

It's for <sup>say name(s) of</sup> <sup>your child(ren).</sup>
It's for me too!

Mark 1:16-20;
2:13-14;
John 1:43-51

4

Everywhere Jesus went, people needed to hear about God. So many people wanted to listen to Jesus.

Jesus looked around for someone to help him. He found fishermen Peter and Andrew in their boat. "Follow me!" said Jesus.

"Yes, we will! We'll help!" said Peter and Andrew, the fishermen.

But two helpers weren't enough. Jesus found fishermen James and John fixing their nets. "Follow me!" said Jesus.

" **Y**es, we will! We'll help!" said James and John, the fishermen.

Jesus needed more than four helpers. He found Matthew, the money man. "Follow me!" said Jesus.

"Yes, I will! I'll help!" said Matthew, the money man.

Five fine helpers—but Jesus kept looking. He found Philip, the friendly one. "Follow me!" said Jesus.

"I will! I'll help!" said Philip, the friendly one.

Philip brought his friend Nathanael to Jesus. "I want to follow you too," Nathanael told Jesus. "For I know that you are God's own Son."

One

Seven

Two

Eight

Three

Nine

Four

Ten

Five

Eleven

Six

Twelve!

Twelve times Jesus said, "Follow me!" And twelve men said, "Yes, we will be your helpers! We'll help you tell everyone about God's love!"

wonder if you know that God loves you too . . .

---

*Dear God, thank you for people who help tell everyone about your love. We're glad you love us too. Amen.*

# Suggestions for Follow-up

## Opening

During your time together today, watch for opportunities to praise your little helpers. Let them know you are pleased—and so is Jesus—when they share a toy, pick up a mess, wait for a turn, or help a friend. Tell them that Jesus needs many helpers to show God's love to others, and they can be Jesus' helpers too.

## Learning Through Play

Learning through play is the best way! The following activity suggestions are meant to help you provide props and experiences that will invite the children to play their way into the Scripture story and its simple truth. Try to provide plenty of time for the children to choose their own activities and to play individually. Use group activities sparingly—little ones learn most comfortably with a minimum of structure.

1. Set up a "fishing pond" for dramatic play. You can use a child's wading pool and make fishing poles from dowels, heavy cord, and large paper clips. Cut fish from colored posterboard and attach a strip of magnetic tape to each. If you wish, set out waders, old hats, small nets, and tackle boxes, and encourage the children to pretend they are Peter, Andrew, James, and John. Watch carefully to make sure that poles are kept away from faces, and help each child catch at least one fish. Remind your little ones that Jesus' helpers left their fishing to help Jesus tell about God's love.

2. Suggest that the children pretend it is Sunday. Tell them they can be Jesus' helpers by inviting their friends to come to church with them. You may want to form a worship circle and sing "Jesus Loves Me" (Songs Section, *God Loves Me* program guide) or other favorite songs together.

3. Set out supplies for making greeting cards. Cut sheets of construction paper in half, and then fold in half again. On the inside write God Loves You. Provide heart-shaped and other pretty stickers, and let children decorate the cards to give or send to a family member or friend. Ask your little ones to decide who they'd like to give their card to, and remind them to do so! Praise them for helping Jesus tell someone about God's love.

4. Invite your little ones to play "Follow the Leader." You may need to take a turn as leader first, and then ask for volunteers to lead the action. If there is a child with special needs in your group, be sure to think of ways this little one can participate too. You can sign actions, imitate sounds, or use only hands and no feet. When the children are ready for a rest, talk about what it means to follow Jesus. Give examples of things little ones can do.

5. Invite your little ones to mimic your actions as you say this action rhyme:

> *When Jesus saw the fishermen* (hold one hand over eye)
> *in boats upon the sea,* (cup hands together for boat)
> *he called to them,* (cup hands around mouth)
> *"Come leave your nets,* (motion to come)
> *and follow, follow me."* (walk in place)
>
> —Words: W. L. Jenkins, © 1953, renewed 1981. From *Songs and Hymns for Primary Children*. Used with permission of Westminster John Knox Press.

## Closing

Sing several of these stanzas of "God Is So Good" (Songs Section, *God Loves Me* program guide) as children follow your actions:

> *God is so good . . .* (point up)
> *He loves me so . . .* (cross hands over heart)
> *I'll follow him . . .* (hold hands and walk in a row)
>
> —Words: Stanza 1, traditional

Place a heart sticker on each child's hand as they leave, and whisper, "God loves you."

### At Home

Spend some time with your child making a personal reminder to follow Jesus. Trace your child's hands and feet on colored paper, cut them out, and glue them to a larger sheet of paper. Or pour washable tempera paint into a shallow pan, and let your little one dip hands and feet into the paint and make handprints and footprints on a large sheet of paper. You might want to make this a family project outside with a hose handy for cleanup. Title your poster Following Jesus. Or use fabric paint to make the prints and caption on a T-shirt for your child. While you work together, talk about ways your child can follow Jesus. Suggest being kind to others, helping around the house, and other simple ways appropriate for your little one.

## Old Testament Stories

**Blue and Green and Purple Too!** *The Story of God's Colorful World*

**It's a Noisy Place!** *The Story of the First Creatures*

**Adam and Eve** *The Story of the First Man and Woman*

**Take Good Care of My World!** *The Story of Adam and Eve in the Garden*

**A Very Sad Day** *The Story of Adam and Eve's Disobedience*

**A Rainy, Rainy Day** *The Story of Noah*

**Count the Stars!** *The Story of God's Promise to Abraham and Sarah*

**A Girl Named Rebekah** *The Story of God's Answer to Abraham*

**Two Coats for Joseph** *The Story of Young Joseph*

**Plenty to Eat** *The Story of Joseph and His Brothers*

**Safe in a Basket** *The Story of Baby Moses*

**I'll Do It!** *The Story of Moses and the Burning Bush*

**Safe at Last!** *The Story of Moses and the Red Sea*

**What Is It?** *The Story of Manna in the Desert*

**A Tall Wall** *The Story of Jericho*

**A Baby for Hannah** *The Story of an Answered Prayer*

**Samuel! Samuel!** *The Story of God's Call to Samuel*

**Lions and Bears!** *The Story of David the Shepherd Boy*

**David and the Giant** *The Story of David and Goliath*

**A Little Jar of Oil** *The Story of Elisha and the Widow*

**One, Two, Three, Four, Five, Six, Seven!** *The Story of Elisha and Naaman*

**A Big Fish Story** *The Story of Jonah*

**Lions, Lions!** *The Story of Daniel*

## New Testament Stories

**Jesus Is Born!** *The Story of Christmas*

**Good News!** *The Story of the Shepherds*

**An Amazing Star!** *The Story of the Wise Men*

**Waiting, Waiting, Waiting!** *The Story of Simeon and Anna*

**Who Is This Child?** *The Story of Jesus in the Temple*

**Follow Me!** *The Story of Jesus and His Twelve Helpers*

**The Greatest Gift** *The Story of Jesus and the Woman at the Well*

**A Father's Wish** *The Story of Jesus and a Little Boy*

**Just Believe!** *The Story of Jesus and a Little Girl*

**Get Up and Walk!** *The Story of Jesus and a Man Who Couldn't Walk*

**A Little Lunch** *The Story of Jesus and a Hungry Crowd*

**A Scary Storm** *The Story of Jesus and a Stormy Sea*

**Thank You, Jesus!** *The Story of Jesus and One Thankful Man*

**A Wonderful Sight!** *The Story of Jesus and a Man Who Couldn't See*

**A Better Thing to Do** *The Story of Jesus and Mary and Martha*

**A Lost Lamb** *The Story of the Good Shepherd*

**Come to Me!** *The Story of Jesus and the Children*

**Have a Great Day!** *The Story of Jesus and Zacchaeus*

**I Love You, Jesus!** *The Story of Mary's Gift to Jesus*

**Hosanna!** *The Story of Palm Sunday*

**The Best Day Ever!** *The Story of Easter*

**Goodbye—for Now** *The Story of Jesus' Return to Heaven*

**A Prayer for Peter** *The Story of Peter in Prison*

**Sad Day, Happy Day!** *The Story of Peter and Dorcas*

**A New Friend** *The Story of Paul's Conversion*

**Over the Wall** *The Story of Paul's Escape in a Basket*

**A Song in the Night** *The Story of Paul and Silas in Prison*

**A Ride in the Night** *The Story of Paul's Escape on Horseback*

**The Shipwreck** *The Story of Paul's Rescue at Sea*

## Holiday Stories

Selected stories from the New Testament to help you celebrate the Christian year

**Jesus Is Born!** *The Story of Christmas*

**Good News!** *The Story of the Shepherds*

**An Amazing Star!** *The Story of the Wise Men*

**Hosanna!** *The Story of Palm Sunday*

**The Best Day Ever!** *The Story of Easter*

**Goodbye—for Now** *The Story of Jesus' Return to Heaven*

These fifty-two books are the heart of *God Loves Me,* a Bible story program designed for young children. Individual books (or the entire set) and the accompanying program guide *God Loves Me* are available from CRC Publications (1-800-333-8300).